Parenting Econ~~omy~~

How to be Financially Stable in an
Unstable World

By: Patrick Baldwin

Copyright 2017
American Christian Defense Alliance, Inc.
Baltimore, Maryland
ACDAInc.Org

Special Request

Thank you for purchasing our book and supporting our Ministry. We actually have two requests – To Pray for Our Ministry and to Read this Book All the Way through. No Ministry can Survive without Prayers and Support so we ask you to keep our Ministry in Your Daily Prayers and Pray as the Lord leads.

We encourage you to Read the Book you purchased all the way through. Many Books NEVER Get Read, and the ones that do only get read the first few pages.

One of our Special Request is that if you are serious about learning the material in this book that you take time to actually read this book in its entirety – all the way through.

We all lead such busy lives nowadays and can get side tracked so easily, please take a moment to consider my words and read to the end of the book and keep us in Your Prayers.

Thank You once again for purchase. We deeply appreciate Your Prayers and Support and know that God will Bless You as You continue to Bless this Ministry.

Dedication

This book is dedicated to every parent out there that has ever struggled to make ends meat yet never gave up. You are an inspiration to us all and prove that hard work truly does pay off.

God Bless Each of You.

Forward

Do you recognize any of these songs about money?

"Money, money, money...must be funny in the rich man's world. Money, money, money, always sunny in the rich man's world." (ABBA)

"Can't buy me love...can't buy me love...I don't care too much for money, 'cause money can't buy me love." (The Beatles)

"If you've got the money, honey, I've got the time...." (Lefty Frizzell)

ABBA's song believes money makes life happy and grand.

Lefty Frizzell's song puts monetary value on friendship and love by singing he only wants to spend time with someone who can show him a good time materialistically.

The Beatles, however, got it right on this one. Money can't buy love or anything associated with it (happiness, success, or fulfillment).

What about these quotes on the subject of money? Have you heard any of these before?

We can tell our values by looking at our checkbook stubs. ~Gloria Steinem

Ms. Steinem and I don't agree on much of anything else, but we do agree on this. Looking at a person's checkbook (or online statement, these days) tells you exactly where their values and priorities lie.

When your outgo exceeds your income your upkeep is your downfall. ~Author unknown, c.1945

Obviously not much has changed since 1945 when it comes to the problem of trying to live above our means. Will we ever learn?

It's a kind of spiritual snobbery that makes people think they can be happy without money. ~Albert Camus

Mr. Camus, I feel sorry for you…very sorry. I don't just think I can be happy without money. I *know* I can be happy without money. Happiness in its true state can't be had or found. It is a state of being.

When I was young I thought that money was the most important thing in life; now that I am old I know that it is. ~Oscar Wilde

Mr. Wilde, I feel sorry for you, as well. You wasted your life and your God-given talent living in a way and writing works that dishonored God. You died at an early age; miserable, destitute, and without any of the money you thought was so important.

"Your money, or your life." We know what to do when a burglar makes this demand of us, but not when God does. ~Mignon McLaughlin

I'm not going to comment on this quote, only to say that God has already demanded this from each of us. And now I'll ask, what was your response?

I had an economics teacher that said money is nothing more than a means of exchange for the goods and services we want. But, she added, the problem a lot of people have in dealing with money is that they come to believe that the amount of money they have is a measure of their entitlement to those goods and services.

In other words, what she was saying is that people tend to equate money with human worth - WRONG!

God, being the creator and master ruler of the universe, has some very definite expectations and commands for us when it comes to well, everything...including money.

But He also knows that because we are wired the way we are and because we live in a sinful world, the issue of money is one that has the potential to cause some serious problems in our marriages and in our homes. And for whatever reason, these problems tend to escalate when we bring the added responsibility of children into the picture.

The purpose of this book, therefore, is to help you, as parents, to get a clear and accurate Biblical-perspective and focus on your finances. In reading this book you will be encouraged to view, handle, and spend money God's way. You will also hopefully come to realize that while money is a necessity for being a responsible citizen in society, it is not something you should put your faith in. It is, as simply a means to an end.

I want to ask that you take a minute to pray before continuing your reading. Pray that God will loosen the grip you have on your money in order to tighten your grip on His leading hand.

Table of Contents

Chapter 1: Financially Stability

What is financial stability? When I posed this question to some of my friends and acquaintances on social media, here are some of the responses I got:

Financial stability is having enough to pay the bills without thinking you don't.

It's not having to feel guilty for your daily trip thru the Starbucks drive-thru.

Financial stability is a state of mind.

I'll let you know when I figure it out.

I agree with the person who said financial stability is a state of mind. We feel financially stable, but a lot of people would feel like they were living in poverty if they 'had to survive' on our income.

Financial stability is using your credit card to get the points—all the while knowing when the bill comes you can pay it in full.

Financial security is not having to look at your bank account every day because you know there's enough to cover everything...and then some.

I don't really know because I've never felt like I was.

It's knowing how much you have coming in and making that be enough.

To be financially secure means to spend less than you make so that when you make less you'll still have something to spend.

I really can't find fault with any of those answers. But there is one core or foundational money-fact not mentioned by anyone. It is the fact that our money (and everything else we have, for that matter) is not really ours. It all belongs to God. He is only letting us borrow it.

Now I know for a fact that many, if not most of the people who responded to my question live in such a way that honors and acknowledges God as the true owner of their money and material blessings. They tithe their income. They share their material blessings. They give of their time and talents to serve God and others. And it is **because they are faithful and obedient to God's commands and expectations concerning money that they enjoy financial stability.**

Something else I know is that it's always easy to let go of our anxieties and the stress we feel over money-matters—especially when you are dealing with decisions about whether or not having a baby (or another baby) is financially responsible, whether to be a stay-at-home-mom or not, how you are going to pay for the food, clothes, and all the other stuff they need now *and* save for their college education. I get it—it's enough to make your faith get the quivers. I know because I've been there.

But I can tell you for sure and for certain that it's always better to throw a blanket of trust over that quivering faith instead of jumping into a fire that ends up burning you instead of warming you. The blanket of trust I'm talking about is the blanket that gives God control over your finances so you don't have to worry about them.

God's financial security blanket

God promises over and over again in his Word to take care of us—to provide for us. In return for fulfilling that promise he asks only one thing of us. He asks that we trust him *completely.*

Being wrapped in God's financial security blanket requires us to exhibit our trust by tithing.

Tithing is the act of giving *back* to God ten percent of everything we have. That's all— just ten percent. You pay almost that much in sales tax just to be able to purchase a new pair of jeans, that new set of golf clubs, or the remote-control car your son has been asking for, for his birthday.

Tithing isn't a suggestion or a good idea. Tithing is a command from God...

(God speaking to Moses) *And all the tithe of the land, whether of the seed of the land, or of the fruit of the tree, is the Lord's: it is holy unto the Lord. (Leviticus 27:30)*

Moreover, in Malachi 3:8-10, God tells the Israelite nation that they are robbing him by not tithing. This pronouncement of guilt is immediately followed, though, by a challenge or dare from God....

Will a man rob God? Yet ye have robbed me… Bring ye all the tithes into the storehouse, that there may be meat in mine house, and prove me now herewith, saith the Lord of hosts, if I will not open you the windows of heaven, and pour you out a blessing, that there shall not be room enough to receive it.

Tithing is the epitome of financial responsibility. When you tithe you are saying you have complete trust in God…about everything. When you tithe you are saying you realize you are only a caretaker of God's wealth. When you tithe you are saying you want to be the recipient of the full measure of blessings God wants to give you.

Tithing doesn't reduce your income. It adds to it. I know that sounds backwards, but it's true. Ask anyone who tithes. They will tell you without exception that they have never been unable to pay a bill or cover their necessary expenses.

They may not be driving a Lexus or taking exotic vacations, but they also don't care about those things. They are experiencing the freedom to live without financial stresses and hardships. And that, my friend, is worth more than all the money in the world.

Chapter 2: Two-Income Families

If you are in your twenties or thirties you are most likely either a) thinking about starting a family, b) just starting your parenting journey, or c) elbow-deep in the joys and chaos of raising your children.

I'm also confident in saying that every single one of you have asked yourself and your spouse the question of whether or not you should be a one or two-income family.

Are children raised in homes with stay-at-home-moms (or dads) really better off?

Are children who don't go to preschool at an academic disadvantage when they start school?

Are the costs incurred with being a two-income family really worth the hassle and effort?

If I stay at home with my children am I wasting my education?

Will we be able to make ends meet with just one income when we barely do it now with two?

Is it a sin to work outside the home instead of staying home with the kids?

If I have the option of working at home, is it possible to do that and still give my kids the attention they need and deserve?

These are all legitimate questions for couples to ask themselves *and* each other. Most of them are also questions with more than one right answer, depending on your particular situation. So for the next few minutes we are going to look at them one at a time and discuss several possible answers. In doing so my hope and prayer is that you will be able to make the best and most God-honoring choices for your family.

Are children raised in homes with stay-at-home-moms (or dads) really better off?

Countless studies have been done on the subject. Results of these studies vary—often times depending on which what those doing the researchers want them to show. That's why it is always best to look at the results of the research done by unbiased entities like the National Institute of Child Health and Human Development, the Pew Research Organization, and the University of Minnesota.

Researchers with these and other similar organizations have nothing to gain or lose regardless of the results. Here is what their research proved:

Children who grow up in daycare facilities have higher levels of stress, are more physically aggressive (a greater tendency to bully), and are have a lower sense of self-worth and self-esteem.

A study done at Stanford University shows that children of stay-at-home-moms fare better academically, socially, and personally—both as children and adolescents—than their peers who spend their days in childcare.

It should be noted, though, that children whose daycare situation is to spend the day with Grandma or another family member, or who have an in-home caregiver are better off than those in a traditional daycare setting.

Now let's take a look at the situation from a parent's perspective...

Research from these unbiased entities show that over sixty percent of parents in America say they firmly believe that children raised in a stay-at-home-parent situation fare much better than those who don't. NOTE: this sixty percent includes parents who work outside the home.

These beliefs are starting to show in the choices parents are making. While the number of stay-at-home-moms (or dads) has been on the rise since the 1940's, it is now beginning to trend downward. That's right— more parents are choosing to have one parent (usually Mom) stay at home full-time with the kids instead of relying on daycare.

Are children who don't go to preschool at an academic disadvantage when they start school?

The answers to this question aren't as varied as those in the previous question. And the keyword in this question is *preschool* vs. daycare.

Daycare is typically considered a place where children are provided meals, naps, a safe place to play, and someone to watch over them in a loving manner while they are doing those things.

Preschool, on the other hand, is more of teaching/learning environment. We use the two words to mean the same thing, but technically, they aren't.

There is no denying the fact that children need to be prepared to go to school. It's *how* they are prepared and to *what extent* they are prepared that causes the rift or debate on the subject.

When we talk about being prepared for school I'm not talking about knowing how to spell and write their name. I'm also not talking about already knowing how to read, recognize site words, and other such academic milestones. That's what they go to school *for*.

When we talk about being prepared to go to school, children need to know how sit still for brief periods of time; focusing on a task.

They need to know how to listen without interrupting, share, understand basic concepts such as opposites, shape recognition, basic counting, and recite the alphabet. They need to be able do their own self-care in the bathroom, tell someone their name, their parents' names, their address, and their phone number. Children also need to know how to dress themselves, feed themselves, hold a conversation, use their manners, and they need to have reached the normal standards recognized by the medical community in regards to fine and gross motor skills.

I personally know several stay-at-home-parents whose children are just as prepared (if not more so) to go to school in all of these areas as their 'professionally-preschooled' peers are. These things aren't rocket science. They are common life skills and lessons every parent should be teaching anyway. So no, not going to preschool doesn't put your child at an academic disadvantage.

Ignoring your child or being lax in your job as a parent…that's what puts your child at an academic disadvantage.

Jolene, a mother of four, stayed busy with the kids and working their farm with her husband, John. But she was never so busy that she failed to have 'school time' three days a week. During this hour she and the kids worked on learning the alphabet, counting, opposites, shapes, colors—all of the basics, according to what they were ready for. They learned to recognize and write their names, how to care for themselves, handle scissors, paint brushes, and glue, and they learned a LOT about science by helping on the farm. In other words, these kids were ready for school.

Sharon, on the other hand, did nothing significant to prepare her children for school. She was of the opinion that the only thing children should do until they went to school was play.

While playtime is definitely an essential element of childhood, there is no reason learning cannot and should not be fun. She should have made a portion of their time more structured and purposeful. In doing so her children wouldn't have had to deal with the discipline and learning issues that stemmed from nothing more than a lack of maturity.

That being said, I also know several children who go to preschool—even those who live in a home with a stay-at-home mom or one that works part-time. These children attend preschool for a variety of reasons. For example…

Elaine and her husband are the parents of two girls, ages 4 and 2. Elaine's husband works full time, nine to five. Elaine, who is an RN, works two twelve-hour night shifts each week. So on those the day of her second shift and the day after that, the girls go to preschool so Elaine can sleep.

Going to the church-operated preschool gives their girls a chance to learn and socialize. The values and Biblical teaching they receive at home and at church is supplemented on these two days, and for their two year-old, whom they adopted from South Korea, the interaction and added necessity to communicate in English has proven to be beneficial.

Joni, a full-time stay-at-home-mom, took both of her children to preschool two half-days a week for a year and a half before they entered kindergarten. She did so partially out of necessity. At this time in her life they were dealing with serious health issues with her mother in-law. The hours the kids were at preschool enabled Joni to bathe her mother in-law, take her to the doctor without having two preschoolers hanging out in waiting rooms, and so forth.

Another view on preschool often comes from parents of special-needs children. Parents of children with special needs often opt for a part-time preschool opportunity for their child in order to give them a safe, structured, and needs-friendly environment to socialize. These preschools can also be a godsend for parents with limited resources when it comes to providing the extra learning tools their child needs.

The final aspect you need to consider regarding preschool is how regimented and aggressive it is. Are they too rigid and structured; allowing little or no free time? Are they pushing children to learn more than they are capable of learning and retaining? Are they encouraging a love for learning or are they trying to turn out little geniuses?

Children's brains can only soak up so much at a time. What's more, their comprehension levels grow with them. You can't make them learn something they aren't ready to learn.

You should know that from doing the whole toilet training thing. In other words, you cannot force a child's brain to learn more than it is capable of. To do so only frustrates the child; making them feel inadequate and causing them to have a disdain for learning and education before they even get started.

The bottom line on preschool is this: If you are really doing your job as a parent, preschool isn't necessary (unless there are special needs or circumstances). But preschool isn't a bad thing, either. It won't hurt your child *as long as* the structure of the program is PRE school… not push-them-to-do-more-than-they-can-school.

Are the costs incurred with being a two-income family really worth the hassle and effort?

If you are asking if the money is ever worth the time spent away from your children and the memories you'll both make, the answer is a great big NO. Never. Never *ever.*

If you are asking whether or not the money made from having two incomes justifies all the added expenses of being a two-income family, there is no real definitive answer. That is something you and your spouse need to decide for yourselves. But since you asked, let's take a few minutes to look at it from a practical dollars and cents point of view.

When you and your spouse both work outside the home there are a number of expenses incurred that wouldn't exist if you (or your spouse) stayed home. Some of these things are obvious:

✓ Professional clothes or uniforms

✓ The money you spend on gas

✓ Cost of public transportation if you use it OR parking fees

✓ The cost of childcare (that's a BIG one)

✓ The cost of food you buy when you are out and about (lunch, coffee, etc.)

In addition to those things there are a lot of not-so-obvious or hidden costs incurred from being a two-income family....

While we readily admit you use more gas in your car, have you considered the fact that your tires wear out quicker? You have to change the oil more often? The added mileage on the car decreases its value sooner, and you actually pay more in car insurance premiums when the car is driven to and from work every day vs. being classified as a pleasure vehicle.

In addition to the fact that you buy types of clothes when you work outside the home, people usually pay more to have those clothes dry cleaned. People also tend to buy more clothes as well as more expensive clothes and shoes when they work outside the home.

As a general rule, children who spend their days in daycare or preschool spend more time sick than those who don't.

This translates into more doctor visits and more medicine (prescription or OTC). You also know that when your kids bring a cold or virus home it is almost a certainty that everyone in the house will get their turn to be miserable. So that means not only do you end up taking them to the doctor more often and buying them more medicine, but you do the same for you and everyone else in the house, as well.

Not only do you spend more money on food and beverages while working, it has been proven time and again that families in which both parents work outside the home spend more on food overall. They eat out more (usually fast-food). They spend more on grocery items because they buy quick-fix, ready-to-eat, pre-packaged foods that aren't nearly as good for you or nutritionally satisfying.

As you look over these lists of things you are spending money on so you can be gone from home all day, ask yourself how much are you really making...bottom line. Are you realizing enough to justify the time you taking from your family and giving to so many others? If not, then why put yourself and your family through the hustle and bustle and chaos of juggling schedules and having such a limited amount of time together?

If in fact you are making a substantial financial contribution to your family, I would encourage you to ask yourself:

Is a career outside the home while your children are young so important?

Are these other people more important than your children?

If I stay at home with my children am I wasting my education?

No. I don't care what your degree is in, there is absolutely nothing more important in life than raising your children to be happy, healthy, well-adjusted, socially-conscious, God-fearing/loving, human beings. Besides, you can either put your education to use in the workforce once the kids are older, or get creative in how you use it while they are still young (more on that later on).

Will we be able to make ends meet with just one income when we barely do it now with two?

This question is closely tied to the question of whether or not it's worth the effort and hassle to be a two-income family. And like that question, there is no one solution that is right for everyone. One thing I will say, however, is that where there's a will there's a way. The human heart and mind is one that thrives on determination. If we really want something bad enough...we'll find a way to make it happen.

Keeping that in mind, if you are 'only' dealing with the normal everyday expenses of living (rent/mortgage, utilities, groceries, and so forth) then I'm going to say that there are most likely several things you can do to cut expenses and make it work on just one income.

If, however, you are carrying a large amount of student loan debt or have a significant monthly expense due to circumstances beyond your control (medical expenses not covered by insurance, special care required for a family member, or the added responsibility of caring for elderly parents, for example), you may need to work up to being a one-income family. It might need to be something you set as your goal.

We're going to cover this more thoroughly in the next chapter, so keep reading and hopefully you will be able to implement some of the suggestions made for paring down your expenses so that you can increase both the quality and quantity of your family's time together.

Is it a sin to work outside the home instead of staying home with the kids?

No. Nowhere in the Bible does it say it is a sin for a mother to work outside the home.

If I have the option of working at home, is it possible to do that and still give my kids the attention they need and deserve?

Yes. It is most definitely possible. We will cover this subject in greater detail in another chapter.

Being a two-income family may or may not be right for you, but before you make that decision, make sure you have all the facts, run all the numbers, and count all the costs.

Chapter 3: Paring it Down

Proverbs 17:1 says:

Better is a dry morsel, and quietness therewith, than an house full of sacrifices with strife.

The more modern way of saying this might be, "money can't buy happiness".

All one has to do is turn on the news or look online to know that the world we live in has more than its share of selfish, greedy, and even evil people. But I am also hear to say that there are a lot of really awesome, Godly people out there—including you.

It is also very encouraging to me to see and hear that more and more of these awesome people are realizing that money and material possessions aren't nearly as important as previously believed.

More and more young adults are turning their noses up (in a good way) at the lifestyle they were raised in—the big sprawling house, all the latest luxuries and gadgets, and a massive closet full of expensive clothes and accessories.

Oh, don't get me wrong. I'm not naïve. I know there are still far too many people out there that believe they need these things. But the retail economy, the housing market trends, and the number of people blogging and tweeting about 'downshifting' their life is very telling. And what it is telling society is that want to live differently than their parents do. They want to live more simplistically. The words 'minimalism', 'downshifting', 'natural', 'sustainable', and 'alternative' are used quite often by people embracing this not-so-new-new way of living. And would you like to know why? Because it works and because it is so physically, emotionally, and spiritually satisfying and gratifying, that's why.

Paring down to live it up is simply getting rid of the excess and the unnecessary distractions in your life *so that you can* have more time and energy to give to those things that really matter. I'm not talking dirt floors, outdoor plumbing, and making your clothes out of worn-out bed sheets. I'm talking about taking a look at your bank account to see what your priorities really are and then doing whatever is necessary to get them (your priorities) where they need to be.

The following suggestions are things that have been proven to be beneficial to families who truly have the desire to grow closer to the LORD and to one another. My prayer is that you will take them to heart; giving yourselves and your children a life-long lesson in knowing what is really important in life.

Tithe first. We spent quite a bit of time in the first chapter talking about tithing, but it really is an essential element of being financially stable and secure.

By recognizing and acknowledging that we are merely stewards of God's wealth, which is best done by tithing, we are freeing ourselves from the temptation of placing our faith in money and material possessions.

Tithing is also a form of worship—the very thing we were created to do. And when we do what we were created to do, we are more stable, secure, and content.

Housing. Part of our job as parents is to provide our children with a safe and secure place to live. That doesn't mean, however, that everyone has to have their own bedroom and bathroom. Countless families with four, six, ten, or even more children grew up sharing a bedroom (and even a bed) with their siblings.

Get rid of your big house. A family of four can do just fine in a house with a thousand square feet (or possibly even less). Mobile homes and tiny houses are also viable options for a lot of families.

The money saved in mortgage payments, taxes, and insurance can pay for your kids' college education! No, seriously, it can.

Remember: space (as in square footage) creates distance (as in not communicating or knowing someone). Parents who give their children a lot of space often end up being so distanced from them they never really know them.

If you're looking into RVing Full-Time Anthony J. Fleischmann Jr. published a great Book that I highly recommend called, "How to Finance Your Full-Time RV Dream". This book offers some great advice on saving money while RVing Full-Time to working from the road online. A must have book for anyone considering living and working while RVing Full-Time.

Transportation. Every family needs reliable transportation. You are never money ahead to buy a car that you can't count on and one that costs you time and money every time you turn around. On the other hand, you don't need a vehicle equipped with luxury options galore. All you need is a reliable vehicle that will accommodate your family's size.

If you are driving high-dollar vehicles, trade down. The money you save on car payments, insurance, and taxes can provide you with the funds necessary to take your family on a nice, yet simple vacation.

Or better yet consider RVing Full-Time and save money on a Family Vehicle and Housing at the same time – Can you tell I really like the idea of RVing, that's because it makes so much sense in today's world.

Clothes, books, and toys. We need clothes. We need books. And yes, we even need toys. What we don't need, though, is an abundance of any of them. We also don't need the most expensive options available.

Kids don't need designer clothes. They need quality clothes that are durable, easy to wear and easy to clean. There are some high quality mid-priced brands that can do the job—brands that are readily available in-store or online no matter where you live. For older kids, one or two nicer things (name-brand shoes, jeans, or a special shirt) make great gifts that fulfill a need for tweens and teens to feel like they fit in.

Kids need books. Books inspire creativity and imagination. Books encourage learning and a love for education. Books entertain. Books teach you something new. Books make you think and inspire you to dream and aspire. Kids need books to call their own. But a library card is a wonderful thing and can reduce the clutter in your house.

Once more, libraries offer so many fun programs for kids as well as adults. They offer story times, book clubs, craft and hobby classes, and so much more.

Kids need toys. They need toys that require them to use their imagination and creativity, toys that require them to think (games), and toys that teach. But again, kids don't need a lot of toys.

To reduce the amount of clutter caused by toys, books, and clothes, sell the things they don't need or have a sincere attachment to. Use the money to purchase a family membership to a family museum, season passes to local theater productions, or fitness center. Giving your children the gift of experiences such as these reduces clutter and motivates you to spend time together as a family.

Groceries. One of the biggest drains on a family's budget is food. We have to eat, but most people could drastically reduce the amount of money they spend on food if they would a) eat healthier b) cook c) shop smarter, and d) grow their own food.

You can save money when you **eat healthier** because fresh foods are cheaper than processed foods. For example if you buy a 48 oz. container of plain instant oatmeal and a bag of brown sugar, you will spend between four and five dollars and have forty-eight servings of oatmeal sweetened with brown sugar. If, however, you purchase the pre-made packets of oatmeal and brown sugar, you will pay between three to four dollars for twenty servings. This means that you would spend close to ten dollars for forty-eight servings from pre-made packets! The pre-made packets also contain more sugar than necessary and preservatives—something neither the plain oatmeal or plain brown sugar have.

Pre-packaged and instant foods are more expensive because every process involves cost and the greater the cost to make it shelf-ready, the greater the cost to the consumer. These foods also have chemicals and dyes to keep them looking pretty; something natural and fresh foods do all on their own.

When people **cook** the only costs involved are the food and the minimal amount of electricity or gas it takes to prepare the food. When you eat out, you are paying for the food itself, as well as a portion of the buildings upkeep and the salaries of the workers. For example…the quarter-pound burger you pay three to five dollars for at a fast-food place (not counting the fries) can be cooked at home for just over two dollars (using a higher quality of meat). Homemade pizzas are less than half the cost of having one delivered to your front door.

Being a **smart shopper** is the only way to go no matter what you are shopping for. When it comes to being a smart shopper you need to think and look farther than your big-box grocery stores. Remember, it's not always where you shop that matters. It's *how* you shop.

Take the time to **look at weekly sale ads**. Either shop there or shop at a store that price-matches their competitor's ads. **Use coupons** you clip from magazines or newspapers or print them from online coupon sites. Shop at stores where you can earn loyalty points and rewards. I earn a lot of free items and save a lot of money this way. Stores often reward their loyalty 'club' members by giving them discounts they don't offer to anyone else. Don't cringe when you read this next one: **give stores your email address.** What's more, give it to them every time you shop there. Why? Because a lot of stores track your email address to your shopping habits with them and reward you for your loyalty.

The more times your email address is entered, the better the coupons and perks you receive. NOTE: Set up an email account solely for this purpose. EXAMPLE: momsshoppingmail@mail.com.... Shop at your local **farmer's market.** You'll get the freshest produce, eggs, honey, butter, jams, and herbs you can get. Be careful, though, because some vendors like to make you pay for the 'experience' of buying local.

Grow your own food. Even if you don't have a big yard (or any yard at all) and even if you don't know anything about gardening, you can still grow at least some of your own food. Even if it's an herb garden grown in a pot or a patio tomato plant...it's still something. But I guarantee once you try it you'll get hooked and want to do more.

There are countless blogs, books, and websites that can help you learn to grow your own food.

Your local extension office can also help you in learning to garden using raised beds, large containers, and small plots of ground. You might even consider joining a community garden group in your community. Growing your own food greatly reduces the cost of your grocery bill. Seed, water, (they're both cheap), sunshine (that's free), and your time and energy (which is time and energy well spent).

Utility and luxury costs. Cutting out things like cable, realizing you don't have to have a four hundred dollar phone, limiting the number of televisions in your house to one, being more conscientious of turning lights off when you leave a room, and reducing the amount of electricity you use because you've reduced the size of your home are all ways to pare it down so you can live it up.

What is meant by 'living it up'? When you simplify your lifestyle by reducing or eliminating the amount of stuff you are holding on to, you free yourself to live a life of experiences. Instead of living to pay for designer jeans, a giant-sized mortgage, and a BMW, you live to spend time take relaxing, fun, and educational outings with your family. You live to feel the satisfaction and sense of accomplishment that comes from growing your own food. You live to know from the look on your son's face or the tone in your daughter's voice that something isn't quite right. You live to be able to hear and see God's will for your life and the blessings HE gives because you are depending on him…not the 'almighty' dollar.

So go ahead…pare it down so you can live it up. I promise you won't be sorry.

Chapter 4: Don't Be Afraid Of Money

Over the years I've been given and read quite a bit of advice about money; how to spend it, how to save it, how to perceive it, and how to not be afraid of it.

That last one about not being afraid of money might seem strange to some. But the truth of the matter is that a lot of people (possibly even you) are afraid of money. Or more specifically, you are afraid of not having enough money.

At the onset of the Great Depression thousands of people (primarily men) committed suicide because they lost all their money and were too afraid of living without it.

What was ironic, though, was that most of the men who did this didn't really even have the money to begin with. It was all 'on paper'—investments in the stock market. In other words, they killed themselves because they were afraid of not having something they really didn't have in the first place.

How sad is that?!

The flip-side of that coin (pun intended) can be seen in the woman whose parents were so focused on making money that they never had time for each other or her—their only child. She grew up with everything a person could possibly want in the way of material possessions, but she was both lonely and alone (yes, there is a difference).

She didn't like what money did to people. That is why she decided to do without it as much as possible. She lives a very modest life and allows herself very few comforts in life.

She's afraid that if she lets the pleasures money can buy take root in her heart she won't be able to stop; ending up like she was as a child…lonely and alone.

The good news is that there is a happy medium between these two extremes. We don't need to be afraid of money. God expects us to make, have, and use money. It's a huge part of what makes society work. Think about it…

God gave Abraham, David, and Jacob great wealth.

It was Jacob's money that allowed him and his family to survive the horrible drought by buying grain from the Egyptians.

The father in the parable of the Prodigal Son was a very wealthy man. He was also a Godly man.

The Apostle Paul asked the various churches to take up a collection at times to help with the expenses of taking the Gospel to people throughout the known world in their day.

Do you see what I'm getting at? Do you see that you don't need to be afraid of money? You don't need to be afraid of anything or anyone. Why? Because in 2 Timothy 1:7 we read: *For God hath not given us the spirit of fear; but of power, and of love, and of a sound mind.*

By using the sound mind God equips us with we can make sound judgements and decisions about money with a Godly attitude. By recognizing the power and love he pours *into* us so that it can flow out *through* us, we can depend on those two things to know our needs will be met when we see money as just one more of the tools God gives us rather than the means of our survival.

So remember...

Money isn't something you need to be afraid of. See it for what it is, use it how it is meant to be used, and keep it in its place by refusing to allow it to take up residence in your heart.

Chapter 5: It Is Not A Sin To Be Rich

Nowhere in the Bible does it say it is a sin to be rich. Abraham was rich. David was rich. Solomon was rich. Jacob was rich. The Prodigal Son's dad was rich. The Good Samaritan was rich. But guess what else these people were? Godly. Not perfect, but Godly. Even Solomon, who wandered about as far away from God as one can get, found his way back and realized that everything he had in the way of material possessions was nothing compared to what he had with God.

Other everyday people have been blessed with significant material wealth. But none of them see their wealth as theirs or something they need to hold on to in order to keep it from slipping away. All of these people either have or are currently giving great portions of their wealth to the local ministries.

They do so to enable those who are committed to full-time ministry to focus solely on winning lost souls to Christ and discipling new believers in the Faith. They give generously out of a pure heart and a sincere desire to help those in need. They know that it is only because of what God has given them that they are able to give.

The key to being a Christian with money is —priorities and perceptions. So while the Bible says nothing about wealth being a sin, it still has plenty to say about where a Christian's priorities and perceptions of money need to be. Let's look…

For the love of money is the root of all evil: which while some coveted after, they have erred from the faith, and pierced themselves through with many sorrows. ~1 Timothy 6:10

One of the most popular and most misquoted verses in the Bible. It's the love of…not the money that is the problem.

Those who have wealth and misuse it or place their trust in it will always be disappointed and disillusioned.

He that loveth silver shall not be satisfied with silver; nor he that loveth abundance with increase: this is also vanity. ~Ecclesiastes 5:10

When money is your god you will never have enough of it. You will never be satisfied because only the one true God can offer true satisfaction and contentment.

A good man leaveth an inheritance to his children's children: and the wealth of the sinner is laid up for the just. ~Proverbs 13:22

See? It's not wrong to save and leave your children a monetary inheritance. But the monetary inheritance should be secondary to the spiritual inheritance you leave them of teaching them to know and love Christ as their personal LORD and Savior.

But if any provide not for his own, and specially for those of his own house, he hath denied the faith, and is worse than an infidel. ~1 Timothy 5:8

We have also been commanded to provide for our family. As parents it is YOUR job to make sure they are clothed, fed, and sheltered. Failing to do so is a sin.

If you have been blessed with abundant wealth, or even with above-average wealth, don't apologize. Don't be ashamed. Just make sure that acquiring and maintaining the wealth doesn't come with the price tag of neglecting God and your family according to God's commands and ideals as to what that neglect looks like.

Chapter 6: The Jesus-Style of Living

We know Jesus was a carpenter by trade, but other than that we really have no insight as to how he supported himself during his ministry. We know that at least four of the twelve disciples were fishermen by trade and we *do* see them working in conjunction with following Jesus. We know that these men had homes and that some had families; specifically Peter, whose mother in-law was healed by Jesus.

But where did Jesus stay as he traveled from town to town? How did He earn money for food? We know He did eat—He had to. But where did the money come from? Did He do carpentry work on the side? Did He depend on the disciples' income from fishing and whatever the other guys did? Did He just miraculously always have what He needed? Did He depend on the generosity of others?

And what about a place to stay? Matthew 8:20 tells us He didn't have a place to call home. He was Nomad-Like in the fact that He traveled from town to town never staying long in any one place.

The Bible makes it pretty clear that there were women of faith that followed Jesus and ministered to His needs, most likely providing meals and resources "for the work of the Ministry"

So when the centurion and those with him, who were guarding Jesus, saw the earthquake and the things that had happened, they feared greatly, saying, "Truly this was the Son of God!" ***And many women who followed Jesus from Galilee, ministering to Him***, *were there looking on from afar, . . . ". ~ Matthew 27:54-56*

Other times when Jesus was tested regarding taxes God Himself provided the money – Straight from the Fish's Mouth.

When they had come to Capernaum, those who received the temple tax came to Peter and said, "Does your Teacher not pay the temple tax?" He said, "Yes." And when he had come into the house, Jesus anticipated him, saying, "What do you think, Simon? From whom do the kings of the earth take customs or taxes, from their sons or from strangers?" Peter said to Him, "From strangers." Jesus said to him, "Then the sons are free. Nevertheless, lest we offend them, go to the sea, cast in a hook, and take the fish that comes up first. And when you have opened its mouth, you will find a piece of money; take that and give it to them for Me and you." ~ Matt. 17:24-27

By the way – Jesus corrected Peter in these verses and informed him that the, "Sons are Free" from paying taxes – why do you think that is . . . Because we are part of God's Kingdom and Sons and Daughters of the Most High – Free!

Additionally we see from Scripture that there was one person who was appointed to handle all the money - Judas Iscariot. Unfortunately it was his LOVE of Money that caused him to betray Jesus. It was only after he betrayed Jesus that he realize 30 pieces of Silver wasn't worth it.

But one of His disciples, Judas Iscariot, Simon's son, who would betray Him, said, "Why was this fragrant oil not sold for three hundred denarii and given to the poor?" **This he said, not that he cared for the poor, but because he was a thief, and had the money box; and he used to take what was put in it.** *But Jesus said, "Let her alone; she has kept this for the day of My burial. For the poor you have with you always, but Me you do not have always." ~ John 12:4-8*

"Now after the piece of bread, Satan entered him. Then Jesus said to him, "What you do, do quickly." But no one at the table knew for what reason He said this to him. **For some thought, because Judas had the money box, that Jesus had said to him, "Buy those things we need for the feast," or that he should give something to the poor."**
~ *(John 13:27-29)*

In fact we see a continuation of this form of organization from the Apostles in the Book of Acts:

Now the multitude of those who believed were of one heart and one soul; **neither did anyone say that any of the things he possessed was his own, but they had all things in common.** *And with great power the apostles gave witness to the resurrection of the Lord Jesus. And great grace was upon them all. . . .*

Nor was there anyone among them who lacked; for all who were possessors of lands or houses sold them, and brought the proceeds of the things that were sold, and laid them at the apostles' feet; and they distributed to each as anyone had need.
~ *Acts 4:32-35*

However, this does not mean that God does not provide for His Children directly (even today). There are numerous times in the Bible that God supernaturally intervenes to provide for His family. Some of the more well-known examples include:

Manna and Quails from Heaven

And the Lord spoke to Moses, saying, "I have heard the complaints of the children of Israel. Speak to them, saying, 'At twilight you shall eat meat, and in the morning you shall be filled with bread. And you shall know that I am the Lord your God.'" So it was that quails came up at evening and covered the camp, and in the morning the dew lay all around the camp. . . .

*And when the layer of dew lifted, there, on the surface of the wilderness, was a small round substance, as fine as frost on the ground. So when the children of Israel saw it, they said to one another, "What is it?" For they did not know what it was. And Moses said to them, "This is the bread which the Lord has given you to eat. This is the thing which the Lord has commanded: 'Let every man gather it according to each one's need, one omer for each person, according to the number of persons; let every man take for those who are in his tent.'" Then the children of Israel did so and gathered, some more, some less. So when they measured it by omers, he who gathered much had nothing left over, and he who gathered little had no lack. **Every man had gathered according to each one's need.** ~ Exodus 16:11-18*

Jesus Feeds the Multitudes:

Jesus Feed 5,000 people with five barley loaves and two small fish which was recorded in all four Gospels (Matthew 14:13-21; Mark 6:31-44; Luke 9:12-17; John 6:1-14).

Jesus Feeds 4,000 people with seven loaves of bread and fish, is reported in Matthew 15:32-39 and Mark 8:1-9

Ultimately we have to understand that if we do our part to "Seek the Kingdom of God FIRST and His Righteousness" everything else will work themselves out. Jesus even commands us not to worry about things . . . .

"No one can serve two masters; for either he will hate the one and love the other, or else he will be loyal to the one and despise the other. You cannot serve God and mammon. "Therefore I say to you, do not worry about your life, what you will eat or what you will drink; nor about your body, what you will put on.

Is not life more than food and the body more than clothing? Look at the birds of the air, for they neither sow nor reap nor gather into barns; yet your heavenly Father feeds them. Are you not of more value than they? Which of you by worrying can add one cubit to his stature? "So why do you worry about clothing? Consider the lilies of the field, how they grow: they neither toil nor spin; and yet I say to you that even Solomon in all his glory was not arrayed like one of these. Now if God so clothes the grass of the field, which today is, and tomorrow is thrown into the oven, will He not much more clothe you, O you of little faith? "Therefore do not worry, saying, 'What shall we eat?' or 'What shall we drink?' or 'What shall we wear?' For after all these things the Gentiles seek. For your heavenly Father knows that you need all these things. But seek first the kingdom of God and His righteousness, and all these things shall be added to you. . . . .

Therefore do not worry about tomorrow, for tomorrow will worry about its own things. Sufficient for the day is its own trouble.
~ Matt. 6:24-34

These words spoken by Jesus are His assurance to us that when we put God first everything else…including our money will fall neatly into place.

The Bible also offers a few suggestions on how you can apply the Jesus-style of living to your life in order to become parents who are more family-focused than money-focused.

And whatsoever ye do, do it heartily, as to the Lord, and not unto men; ~Colossians 3:23

When we work with the attitude that we are doing it for the LORD we honor God with what we do and how we do it. We don't neglect our families. Our coworkers, clients, and business associates know who we belong to.

Let your conversation be without covetousness; and be content with such things as ye have: for He hath said, I will never leave thee, nor forsake thee.
~Hebrews 13:5

Know that God will always give you all that you need. Be thankful. Be grateful. Be content.

Remember God never tells us to be idle or lazy. Neglecting your financial responsibilities to your family is no less wrong or sinful than being obsessed with making money – There needs to be a balance in all things.

Remove far from me vanity and lies: give me neither poverty nor riches; feed me with food convenient for me: lest I be full, and deny thee, and say, who is the Lord? or lest I be poor, and steal, and take the name of my God in vain. ~Proverbs 30:8-9

Just enough and no more—this is what the writer of this proverb is asking for. Enough to not question God's promise of provision, but not so much that they forget it is God's generosity that makes their life possible. What more do any of us need?

Remember – The bottom line is this, God's NOT in a Box so Don't TRY to Put Him in One – Expect Great Things from a Great God who Loves YOU1

Chapter 7: What is Failure

Sir James Dyson (the vacuum guy) built over five thousand…yes, thousand prototypes of his famous and hugely successful bag-less vacuum before he finally got it right. Bill Gates dropped out of college to start a business that fell on its face. Walt Disney was fired from a job as a newspaper reporter because the boss said he (Disney) lacked imagination.

Would you consider any of these men failures? I certainly wouldn't! They *experienced* failures, but they *aren't* failures. And neither are you.

When it comes to parenting economics you can rest assured you will make a few mistakes along the way. We all do. I know I've had my share of trying to save a few extra dollars by buying the thing I could find—only to have it fall apart or not work a couple of weeks later.

This, of course, led me to purchasing the quality items I should have purchased in the first place. I saved nothing. And then there are the times I have spent more than I should have on a gift for our child; something they desperately wanted for Christmas. The item never seemed to live up to its expectations though. Either it didn't do what advertisers promised it would or it wasn't near as fun or exciting as my kids thought it would be.

I've also had my share of failed attempts to save money by taking the dollar challenge; setting aside one dollar on the first week of the year, two dollars on the second week…all the way to three hundred and sixty-five dollars on the last week of the year.

I've failed to tithe more times than I want to admit. I've wasted money. I've horded money. But even when you put all of these things together I'm not a failure.

I'm not a failure because I haven't stopped trying. Just like Dyson, Gates, and Disney, I refuse to let my past mistakes dictate my future success. God wants more for me and my family than that. I want more for me and my family than that. Learn from your money mistakes and move forward by seeking God's guidance and direction.

I'm not a failure because I am not wallowing in a sea of 'woe is me'. Don't ever be guilty of or let your children hear or see you blaming someone else for your financial situation. Even if the banks close and you lose it all, don't let this be you, because there's "plenty more where that came from".

That's right—the God who provides, always provides. But His blessings of provision are based on our attitude towards money and our relationship with God. Just like you don't reward your child's bad behavior, God won't reward ours.

So...and I say this with all the love and spirit of Christian brotherhood in the world...if you are suffering financially it MAYBE because you don't have a Godly attitude toward work and money and you aren't trusting God with your finances. When those things change, so to may your financial situation.

I know I'm sounding like a broken record, but the whole entire issue of finances really does boil down to this:

- Our money isn't really ours—God is letting us use it.
- Money is one way God sees our faithfulness and trust towards Him.
- Tithing, which is giving back to God what is His, before we do anything else with the money He lets us use, is the first and most essential step toward financial freedom and blessing.
- The more we trust God, the less important money will be. And the less important money becomes to us, the more God gives us to use and to enjoy.

Priorities and perceptions—that's where it's at. When these two things are in perfect (or near perfect) alignment with God, you will know you are not a failure in God's eyes or in the eyes of your family.

So ask yourself:

Does my work provide my family with more presents than it does my presence?

Can my children say I spend time in conversation or cuddling them (depending upon their age) at least a little while each day?

Have I ever given my children the impression or right to feel they are a financial burden? Have I ever complained about 'having' to buy shoes, clothes, school supplies, etc.?

Do my children hear my spouse and me argue over money?

Do my children spend more time alone at home or in their rooms than they do with us, their parents?

Do my children know what tithing is? Are we teaching them to tithe?

Do I model an attitude of stewardship vs. ownership and greed?

Do I model an attitude that says our worth comes from who we are—not what we have?

When you can answer these questions in a way that proves your priorities and perceptions are in line with the Word of God, you can rest assured that you are NOT a failure.

However, if you're doing everything right according to God's Word and you're still not seeing the Blessings of God you may have a generational curse you are unaware of or have witches coming against you spiritually.

If you're dealing with generational curses that relate to money then you need to plead the Blood of Jesus over your family and finances and Rebuke that generational curse in the Name of Jesus Christ. You may also want to get others involved in praying against this generational curse and for God to open up doors in your life.

During your prayer time don't forget to Bind, Rebuke, and Cast Out the Enemy that may be coming up against you spiritually. Remember Christianity is not just about "Playing Spiritual Defense" it's about getting aggressive with the spiritual enemy and taking back what the devil has stolen – Even more so, advancing the Kingdom of God through "Spiritual Violence". Remember we are in a Spiritual War at all times.

And from the days of John the Baptist until now the kingdom of heaven suffers violence, and the violent take it by force.
~Matthew 11:12

Jesus came to destroy the works of the devil and if you follow Jesus that's your job too! What better place to start then in your own home and with your own family.

Chapter 8: Work and Family

Let's spend a couple of minutes reviewing what you've learned so far about being financially stable in a not-so-stable world...

You have learned that our money isn't really ours—it's Gods.

You have learned that tithing isn't a good idea or something only rich people can afford to do. You have learned that tithing is a command from God.

You have learned that it is not a sin to have money, but rather it's our perception of money that can become a sin in our lives.

You have learned that stuff isn't the stuff love is made of—that love happens only when there is a real and sincere relationship.

You have learned how paring down your expenses allows you to live a fuller life.

You have learned how to pare down those expenses so that you can live a fuller and simpler life.

You have learned that God expects you to provide for your family's financial needs and that failing to do so brings great dishonor to Him.

You have learned that when you are content with what God gives you, you experience true joy and happiness.

You have learned that you are blessed according to your faithfulness—not just with money, but in all things.

That's quite a bit, don't you agree? But we're not done. I want to spend the next few minutes giving your some incredible ideas on how you can work, spend a lot more time with your family, and serve God...all at the same time! I wish I could claim them as my own original ideas, but I cannot.

These are things real people and real families are doing in order to fulfill God's commands to provide for their family, raise their children to know and love the LORD, and to be Jesus to those in need.

These ideas are most definitely ones that can be described as 'thinking outside the box' ideas. Don't let that stop you from seriously considering some of them, though. If it's working for the people who are actually doing them (and it is), then it can work for you and your family, too.

IT works. The 'IT' here meaning *internet technologist.* "Craig", along with his wife and two young daughters, sold their home, one of their cars, and most of their worldly possessions to hit the road for Jesus. They purchased a nice-sized RV to live in and travel around the country so that Craig can set up computer programs for churches and ministry organizations.

He spends two or three days each week working with the staff of the church or organization and then two or three hours the remaining days of the week from the RV; troubleshooting, writing code, and setting appointments.

While "Craig" is working with staff members, his wife home schools the girls. The remainder of the week is spent on school work (2-3 hours a day), playing, sightseeing and learning about the places they are staying, and making new friends.

The fees for "Craig's" services are considerably less than those of larger companies offering these same services, yet after tithing, are sufficient to pay for their living expenses, entertainment, and put some in savings each month.

The doctor or nurse is always in. I know a few people who have chosen to live on the road with their spouse or their spouse and children, while serving God through their profession.

Most of these people travel from community to community (usually low-income or remote desert or mountain communities) to offer medical care for minimal cost. Some even take food, lodging, and hand-made crafts as payment.

One of these women, a nurse, travels across a region of the US with her daughter, offering health screenings to women and children in safe houses. She and her daughter were victims of domestic abuse, so this is her way of giving back. She lives off of grant money and donations, as well as accepting meals and a place to stay from the organizations she serves.

Leaving a legacy. A young husband and father lost his wife in a car accident two years ago. Not wanting to stay in the small community that was full of reminders, this up and coming lawyer took his three year-old son and started a ministry.

He travels across the country giving seminars at churches that help people with legal issues including wills, directives, and setting up businesses to run on Christian principles. Father and son live in their RV and Dad has started homeschooling his son three half-days a week to prepare him for kindergarten next year.

As long as I have internet.... Jane is a freelance writer and a former stay at home mom to her four grown children. Her husband, Tom, is a retired law-enforcement officer. Now the couple travels around the country living for short periods of time in state and national campgrounds. Jane, who writes Christian parenting resources and Bible studies, can work wherever they go. She just has to have internet to submit her work to publishers, which isn't hard to find. The couple is truly enjoying the freedom they have found on the road.

Bob and Vanessa, who became parents at the age of seventeen, along with their seven year-old twins and three year-old, sold nearly everything they had when their youngest children were less than six months old. They put the rest in a pull-behind trailer and in the back of their minivan and moved to New Mexico—the state with nearly a 10% teen pregnancy rate (the highest in the nation). There they set up a school for pregnant teens. The girls come to school three days a week and classes are done online; each girl having their own laptop, desk, and comfortable work station where they can feed, change, and spend time with their baby.

When their babies aren't with them, Vanessa, along with volunteers from a local church, offer an on-site daycare and preschool. Vanessa also homeschools the kids on school days. Bob's responsibilities include proctoring tests, monitoring the girls' progress in keeping up with their assignments, and keeping the laptops in good working order.

Funding for the school and their salaries comes through grants and donations. Bob, Vanessa, and the kids live above the school and can enjoy four days of family time together; part of which includes homeschooling with the entire family taking part.

The options are endless

The options for making a living, raising a family, and serving God in an unconventional way are limitless. It just takes a little imagination, a lot of prayer, and willingness to take that leap of faith once you feel God's leading in any given direction.

Remember If you're looking for a great resource on how to afford RV living check out Anthony J. Fleischmann Jr. book, "How to Finance Your Full-Time RV Dream". I really can't say enough good things about it. It's really a great resource to get you started and in my humble opinion a must have if you plan to RV Full-Time.

Chapter 9: Creative Income Solutions

Selling your house and living in a RV or above a business may not be feasible or even God's calling for you and your family. And that's okay! Not everyone is meant to do the same thing or serve God in the same way. Remember...

For as the body is one, and hath many members, and all the members of that one body, being many, are one body: so also is Christ. For by one Spirit are we all baptized into one body, whether we be Jews or Gentiles, whether we be bond or free; and have been all made to drink into one Spirit. For the body is not one member, but many. If the foot shall say, Because I am not the hand, I am not of the body; is it therefore not of the body? And if the ear shall say, Because I am not the eye, I am not of the body; is it therefore not of the body?

If the whole body were an eye, where were the hearing? If the whole were hearing, where were the smelling? But now hath God set the members every one of them in the body, as it hath pleased him. ~ 1 Corinthians 12:12-18

Equally true is the fact that sometimes it simply is not possible to make it as a single-income family. Or maybe you are the sole provider for your family, but leaving home and therefore leaving your children with someone else isn't an option. Either you cannot afford quality childcare on the salary you make—the salary you have to have in order to have food and shelter—or you are so firmly rooted in your beliefs that a child needs his/her mother that you cannot in good conscience leave them. What to do?

There are actually quite a few viable options for making a good living in the comfort of your own home or at the very least, supplementing your spouse's income.

You just need to make sure that you are willing and able to create a healthy balance of work/home time; something many moms and dads that work from home aren't good at. They end up working more than parenting OR they procrastinate doing their work and it all falls apart. This, of course, depends upon the nature of your work-from-home job.

Working from home is a highly flexible option and one that can, when done correctly, truly give you and your family the best of both worlds, so to speak. Working from home also saves a lot of money on work-related expenses discussed in an earlier chapter of this book.

The following ideas have been tested and are mom, dad, and kid approved, so look over them , decide if any of them are right for you, then take the necessary steps toward becoming more financially stable in the security of your own home.

In-home childcare. This one almost seems hypocritical. You are staying home because you don't want your child raised in daycare, yet here you are offering to do that very thing for others. Hhhmmm....

If your conscience bothers you on this one, yet you feel it is the option that best fits your situation, you might consider offering daycare to single parents who really have little or no choice in the matter. You might also offer childcare to couples who are working different shifts so that one of them can be home with the kids, but whose schedules overlap two or three hours each day. Offering a service like this can provide a much-needed service while supplementing your income and not taking an excessive amount of energy and time away from your family.

Tutoring. Tutoring is a great way to supplement your income or can even earn you a steady, reliable income if you choose to pursue it. There are always going to be children in need of tutoring. Set a scheduled for afterschool and evening hours, get the word out, and you're set. NOTE: I know two couples who quit their teaching jobs to open a tutoring center in the basement of their home. Their own children play in the play area while they tutor individually and in groups of six to ten students.

Music and hobby lessons. This works much like the tutoring situation. Some people I know, however, go to private schools, preschools, and small businesses to teach two or three afternoons or evenings a week. Mom, Dad, Grandma, or some other trustworthy person can watch the kids for you while you work.

Do your thing. Many businesses offer a work-from-home option to their employees rather than losing them altogether. Real estate firms, marketing agencies, interior decorators, insurance companies, and several others service-oriented businesses allow you to work from home. You only have to come in for staff meetings or to make presentations.

Some professions, such as medical bill coding and insurance coding are often done at home. You simply take a training course that lasts a few hours, pass a test to prove you are able to do the work, and then...go to work. Most of the time you can choose how many hours you want to work at these jobs, which is definitely a plus.

Freelancing. Freelancing is also another great option for people who want to work from home. Writing, photography, painting, even mechanical and appliance repair work can be done on a freelance basis. Whatever it is you are good at, do it! And don't worry…when you get the word out that you are available and when your reputation for excellence gets out, you will have plenty of work to keep you busy.

Sales. Women have been selling cosmetics, kitchen storage containers, jewelry, household products, and all sorts of other things at home parties for years. Some are successful at it. Others, not so much. But that really depends upon the individual person and how much effort and energy they are willing to put forth. If you choose to go this route, be sure you are a people person who isn't afraid to say, "Hey, invite your friends over and let me show you some things you will really enjoy!"

BEWARE: Please beware of work-from-home scams. They are everywhere and have caused a lot of people a lot of heartache by depleting their bank accounts and their self-esteem. When choosing to work-from-home, don't pay for anything you cannot tangibly take home on the spot (toys for a daycare, for example) or buy into anything you cannot keep (home party sale demos, for example). You should NEVER pay someone to pay you. Remember – "If it sounds too good to be true, it probably is"

Chapter 10: Final Thoughts on Financial Stability

I think we've just about covered all the basics—tithing, conservativism, paring down to live a simpler, yet more enjoyable life, and even options for creative financial stability. I want to leave you, though, with a few final thoughts on the matter in an effort to encourage you not to let the world's view of money become your own.

Thought #1: Financial stability happens only when you find your *security* in God—not money.

Thought #2: Financial stability requires you to be financially responsible. Being financially responsible means tithing first and providing for your family's needs.

Thought #3: Financial stability means living within your means (not your credit card limits) and being content with what you have.

Thought #4: Financial stability means knowing all you have is simply on loan to you from God and treating it that way.

"Okay, okay!" you say. You get it. I've said it so many times you are beginning to get tired of hearing it. "But," you ask, "if you could sum up *how* to get to this point, what would you say?"

Pray. Ask God to lead you in all your financial decisions. Pray for His wisdom and for humility to never forget that all you have is really His.

Simplify. Get rid of anything and everything that is standing between you and God and you and your family. Bring your family together physically by putting less space (square footage) between you. Bring your family together emotionally and spiritually by spending less time working and more time loving, playing, and serving one another.

Give. Give back to God first. Then after you give your tithe, give your time, talents, and energy to your family and to others. Serve God as a family.

Budget. Create a budget and live within its boundaries.

Change your mind. Spend time each and every day praying for God-eyes when it comes to money and material possessions.

God bless you and your family as you move ever-closer to Him.

Special Gift

God has a Gift for You!   The Plan of
Salvation:

There is no formal prayer of salvation as
many churches would have you believe,
God's Word is very clear - there is only one
way to get to the Father in heaven and that
is through Jesus Christ (John 14:6). Jesus
says that you must be born again to enter
into heaven (John 3:3-5).

Salvation is simply the first step in building
an open and honest relationship with God.
We all have sinned and fallen short, but
there is Hope in Jesus Christ - Just cry out to
God in sincerity and honesty asking for
forgiveness and for Him to Save you,
Sanctify you, and fill you with His Holy Spirit
- Ask for His will to be done in your life on
earth as it is in Heaven and That's it, now
just keep it real with God.

A Warning:

The Christian walk is not an easy life on the surface. The Word of God says that we will be hated in all the world for Christ namesake (Matt. 24:9). The Bible says that in the last days are enemy prevail against us physically until Christ returns to save us (Dan 7:21, 22). Furthermore, we must endure hardship as a good soldier of Jesus Christ (2 Tim 2:3) and yet we are never alone in this, God promises us that He will never leave us nor forsake us if we believe in him (Matt.28:20).

In everything we go through we have the peace and joy of God which surpasses all understanding (Philp. 4:6-8) The Bible declares, "For I consider the sufferings of this present time are not worthy to be compared with the glory which shall be revealed in us". (Rom 8:18). However, in all these things we are more than conquerors through Jesus Christ (Rom. 8:37)

Stay In Contact

Stay in Contact with the American Christian Defense Alliance, Inc. through Our Website At: ACDAInc.Org

Join Our Mailing List

We also Greatly Appreciate You Signing Up For Our Mailing List and Providing a Good Rating and review for this Book. Your reviews help other people like yourself find this book on Amazon and benefit from its contents.

If You or Your Family have been Blessed by this book please let us know by dropping us a line through our website at ACDAInc.Org

Find All Our Books

Some of Our Books:

Parenting: How To Be A Great Parent And Raise Awesome Kids

Wisdom from Your Elders: Learning From Your Parents, Grandparents, and the Older People in Your Church

Salvation for Your Unsaved Mom: 10 Things to Tell Your Mom Before She Dies

Parenting Special Needs Children: A Christian Guide to Parenting Children with ADHD, Autism, Asperger's, and other Psychological, Behavioral, or Physiological Disorders

A Vague Notion: How To Overcome Limiting Beliefs of Fear and Anxiety Through the Word of God

Race Relations in America: A Christian Guide to Help Unite Christians in the Faith

Martial Arts Ministry: How To Start A Martial Arts Ministry

Biblical Bug Out: Don't Bug In - Follow The Calling

Christian Prepping 101: How To Start Prepping

How to Finance Your Full-Time RV Dream

Additional Platforms

Thank you for reading this book. Your support and the support of others continue to enable our Ministry to grow. We hope and pray that this book has blessed you. If you enjoyed this book consider purchasing it on additional platforms or giving it as a gift to someone who could benefit from it.

We have this book available as an E-Book, Paperback, and Audio Book. We have no way to know which platform you purchased our book on but want to make you aware of another way you can help support our Ministry if you haven't yet listen to the audio book version of this book.

If you Enjoy Listening to Audio Books in General Consider Signing Up For Audible.com. If You've Been On the Fence About Signing Up for Audible.com or Would Just like to Support Our Ministry By Purchasing Our Audio Book First – We Would Greatly Appreciate It.

Did You Know that You Can Support Our Ministry By Listening to Our Audio Books on Audible.com?

Here's How:

- Sign Up as a New Aubdible.com Member

- Purchase Our Audio Book First and

- Stay an Audible.com Member for at least 61 Days

If You Follow these Simple Steps Our Ministry will Earn $25.00 -$50.00 Every Time This Process in Completed. The Amount we earn is based on if we have narrated the book ourselves or outsourced it to another narrator.

We Greatly Appreciate Your Support as Well as You Sharing this information, including links to our books on Audible.com with Others on Your Social Media Platforms

Thank You Once Again for Your Support; We Know God Will Bless You as You Have Blessed This Ministry